How to identify female narcissists in 7 steps

Narcissistic Wifes, Volume 3

Dr Paul J Peloquin Sr, PhD

Published by Dr Paul J Peloquin Sr, PhD, 2025.

HOW TO IDENTIFY FEMALE NARCISSISTS IN 7 STEPS

First edition. June 2, 2025.

ISBN: 979-8231871063

Written by Dr Paul J Peloquin Sr, PhD.

Table of Contents

Introduction: The Mask She Wears

They walk among us unnoticed—female narcissists. Not the glamorous vixens of pop psychology or the cruel villains of fiction, but real women who manipulate love, kindness, and empathy like tools in a well-worn toolbox. They smile in public, flatter you in private, and tighten their grip in silence. These women are often successful, persuasive, and admired—but for the men closest to them, life becomes a confusing, painful hell.

This book was born from experience.

I'm Dr. Paul J. Peloquin Sr., PhD— I am not just a doctor of human behavior, but also a man who loved a narcissistic woman for far too long. My relationship started like a dream: intense passion, emotional connection, deep conversations that felt like soul ties. But behind that mask was a woman driven not by love, but by control. Her affection was currency. Her praise, conditional. Her loyalty—fiction.

For years, I excused, justified, and even defended her actions. She wasn't abusive in the obvious way. There were no bruises. But I was bleeding emotionally, drained spiritually, and stripped of my identity. That's what narcissistic abuse does—it makes you doubt what's real. And when the narcissist is a woman, society often fails to believe you. You're the man. You're supposed to be strong. You're supposed to handle it. You're supposed to "man up."

But how do you "man up" when your mind is being twisted daily by a woman who weaponizes love?

This guide breaks that silence.

It isn't clinical. It's not meant to diagnose. It's meant to wake you up, validate your pain, and give you a step-by-step lens to identify her patterns before they become your prison. Because make no mistake—a female narcissist doesn't love you. She uses you. And once she's drained you dry, she'll discard you without a second thought.

You may already be in a relationship with one. You may be recovering. Or maybe, like I once was, you're just starting to realize something isn't quite right.

Either way—this guide is for you.

Let's begin.

Step 1: She Charms First, Controls Later

When you first meet her, it feels like fate.
She's intoxicating.
She's attentive.
She makes you feel like the center of the universe.
You think, finally, someone who sees me.
But beware: this is not love.
It's a performance—and she's been perfecting it for years.

The Narcissistic Love Bomb

Female narcissists begin their control through love bombing: intense displays of affection, attention, and admiration. You receive constant texts, deep eye contact, grandiose compliments, and rapid talk of a future together. "You're not like the others," she says. "I've never felt this before."

It feels amazing—because it's supposed to.

This is how she hooks you. It's not accidental. Her compliments are calculated. Her timing is precise. Her touch is designed to spark chemical addiction in your brain. She is training you to crave her validation.

And just like that, you begin to attach your sense of worth to her opinion.

The Real Purpose Behind Her Charm

What feels like romantic intensity is actually strategic control. Once you're emotionally invested, she begins to subtly test your boundaries:

- She "jokes" about your flaws.
- She questions your friends.
- She criticizes your exes.
- She gauges how easily you will bend to please her.

Every charming moment you replay in your mind—she designed it. Every compliment you hold onto—she weaponizes it later. Charm is not love. For the female narcissist, charm is currency.

Why Men Fall for It

Because we are conditioned to believe that a woman who shows intense interest is simply "more romantic." We confuse intensity with intimacy. We assume we've met someone unusually passionate, rather than someone unusually manipulative.

The female narcissist counts on this misunderstanding. She wears the mask of "dream girl" to disarm your defenses.

And it works—until it doesn't.**Early Warning Signs (Checklist)**

- The relationship escalates extremely fast (moving in, saying "I love you" within weeks).
- She mirrors your interests, values, and language almost perfectly.
- She is overly eager to share "how awful" all her exes were.
- She becomes upset or distant if you pull back or ask for space.
- She asks for a lot of your time and attention, often guilt-tripping when you can't give it.

The Trap

By the time you question her behavior, you're already emotionally hooked. You want the woman you thought she was to come back. You replay the early days, wondering what changed.

But nothing changed.

That early charm wasn't real—it was bait.

How to Break Free from Step 1

Recognize that real love grows steadily. It honors boundaries. It respects your space and your individuality. If a woman seems "too perfect" or moves the relationship at lightning speed, pause. Take a breath. Watch for inconsistencies between her words and actions.

And never confuse attention with affection.

Step 2:

Empathy Is a Performance, Not a Trait

She cries at movies. She volunteers at school. She says she "feels everything deeply."

But when you're hurting? She's cold. Unmoved. Dismissive.

And when you point it out? She says you're the one who's too sensitive.

Welcome to the second trait of the female narcissist: manufactured empathy.

The Mask of Sensitivity

One of the most confusing things about a female narcissist is how emotionally expressive she seems—in public. She might tear up when talking about her childhood, gush over a rescued animal, or play the role of emotional caretaker for others.

But behind closed doors, her reactions don't match your reality.

You could be:

- Exhausted after a hard day
- Devastated by bad news
- Overwhelmed with stress or sadness

And her response?

Indifference. Eye rolls. Or worse—irritation that your emotions are interfering with her needs.

Why? Because female narcissists lack true empathy. What they display instead is performative empathy—used strategically to appear warm, kind, or virtuous when it benefits them.

Empathy becomes just another tool in their toolbox—not a genuine emotion.

Step 3:
Gaslighting Is Her Favorite Weapon

If you've ever walked away from a conversation with her feeling confused, guilty, or like you were losing your mind—congratulations.

You've been gaslit.

Gaslighting isn't a buzzword. It's a psychological weapon. And for the female narcissist, it's her go-to tool for control. She distorts your reality so subtly that you begin to doubt your memories, your emotions, and eventually, your sanity.

What Is Gaslighting?

Gaslighting is emotional manipulation that causes a person to doubt their own perception of reality. The female narcissist uses this constantly—through lies, deflection, blame-shifting, and rewriting history.

When you say:

"That hurt my feelings."

She replies:

"That never happened."

"You're just imagining things."

"You're so sensitive."

"You're always the victim."

Suddenly, instead of addressing the harm she caused, the conversation becomes about your flaws, your reactions, your emotional instability.

And she walks away clean—again.

Why Gaslighting Works So Well

Because you're human. You want to be fair. You want to believe that maybe you misunderstood. You want to keep the peace.

And she knows that.

She uses your empathy against you. She twists facts until your memory seems unreliable. And over time, your inner voice becomes quieter, weaker, and eventually silent.

That silence is her victory.

Common Phrases Narcissistic Women Use to Gaslight

- "You're making things up."
- "That's not how it happened."
- "You always twist my words."
- "You're overreacting."
- "Everyone else agrees with me—you're the only one who thinks that."
- "You're crazy. You need help."

Sound familiar?

These aren't disagreements. These are attacks on your perception. Every time she says one of these, she chips away at your self-trust.

The Cycle of Confusion

Here's how gaslighting typically plays out:

1. You express a need, boundary, or concern.
2. She denies the event or twists it.
3. You try to clarify or explain again.
4. She escalates—either by rage, withdrawal, or mockery.
5. You feel disoriented and begin to question yourself.
6. She acts as if nothing happened—or blames you for being upset.

You begin to think:

"Maybe I am too sensitive."

"Maybe I am remembering wrong."

"Maybe it is my fault..."

This isn't love. This is emotional sabotage.

Real-Life Examples

Let's break it down further:

You: "Last night you said something that really hurt me."

Her: "I never said that. And if I did, you took it the wrong way."

You: "I feel like you're emotionally distant lately."

Her: "That's rich coming from you. You're the one who shuts down."

You: "You've been flirting with someone else."

Her: "You're paranoid. You're imagining things again."

This relentless twisting creates emotional exhaustion—and that's the goal. If you're too confused to stand up for yourself, she wins.

Red Flags You're Being Gaslit

- You apologize constantly—even when you've done nothing wrong.
- You second-guess your memory, reactions, and instincts.
- You feel like "the crazy one" in the relationship.
- You isolate yourself from others out of shame or confusion.
- You dread bringing up issues because the outcome is always your fault.

If you feel like you're losing clarity or doubting your own mind—it's not a coincidence. It's conditioning.

How to Protect Yourself

1. Start a Journal

Write things down as they happen. Date them. Include direct quotes. This creates a paper trail that reminds you what actually happened.

1. Confide in a Trusted Third Party

A friend, therapist, or support group can help you validate your perceptions and restore confidence in your reality.

1. Don't Debate with a Narcissist

You can't reason with someone who is committed to distortion. Protect your energy. Set boundaries instead of engaging in circular arguments.

1. Trust the Confusion

If you walk away from most conversations feeling worse, not better—that's the truth speaking to you. Confusion is the signal, not the problem.

Final Truth:

Gaslighting isn't about disagreement. It's about domination.

And the female narcissist will keep twisting your reality until she's the only source of "truth" in your life.

But here's the real truth:

You're not crazy. You've just been controlled.

Step 4:

She Rewrites Reality to Stay in Control

The female narcissist is not just a manipulator—she's a master storyteller. But the story she tells isn't grounded in truth. It's grounded in power. When facts don't fit her needs, she simply rewrites them.

This is more than lying. It's a form of psychological warfare designed to control how others perceive her—and more dangerously, how you perceive yourself.

The Deliberate Reconstruction of Truth

In the hands of a narcissistic woman, reality is a weapon. She doesn't just bend the truth—she manufactures it. She'll twist timelines, edit conversations, invent motives, and even rewrite your shared history.

Why?

Because controlling the narrative means controlling the power. If she controls the story, she controls the sympathy, the blame, and ultimately—you.

What It Looks Like in Real Life

- You clearly remember a fight that began with her betrayal—but she insists you started it.
- You know she insulted you in front of others—but she denies it and accuses you of embarrassing her.
- She says she "never said that"—even though you recall the conversation vividly.
- She reframes the past with statements like:

"I only acted that way because you pushed me."

"You were never there for me emotionally, so I had no choice."

"I always gave you everything—you just didn't see it."

These aren't different perspectives—they're rewrites of history that serve only her version of reality.

Why This Keeps You Trapped

The more she rewrites, the more you begin to lose track of your own reality.

- You stop trusting your memory.
- You begin defending yourself constantly.
- You try harder to "prove" what really happened.
- You become emotionally exhausted trying to win a game you don't know you're playing.

Eventually, you might start to adopt her version of the past—not because you believe it, but because resisting it is too draining.

That's when she knows she has you.

Reality Distortion in Action

Let's look at how she rewrites real events:

The Event: She flirts with another man at a social gathering.

Your Response: You confront her afterward, calmly.

Her Version: "You embarrassed me in front of everyone by being jealous and insecure. I was just being polite."

The Event: You spend the weekend doing chores and errands.

Her Version (to others): "He never helps me. I do everything alone."

The Event: She emotionally abuses you during a fight.

Her Version: "He yelled at me. I was scared for my life."

She doesn't just tell these stories to you—she tells them to others: friends, family, coworkers, therapists, even the courts. That's why many victims of female narcissists struggle so deeply with isolation: no one else sees the truth.

Why She Does It

1. To Play the Victim

The female narcissist loves to be seen as the wounded woman. Rewriting history allows her to paint you as the villain while she plays the innocent partner who "tried so hard."

1. To Justify Her Abuse

If she can convince herself and others that you were cruel, absent, or unstable, she feels entitled to her toxic behavior.

1. To Control the Narrative

Narcissists fear exposure. The best way to avoid accountability is to control the version of the story everyone hears.

1. To Keep You Disoriented

If you're always trying to defend your memory, you'll never question hers—and that's how she stays in control.

Red Flags

- You often think, "Am I remembering this wrong?"
- You feel like you're being "re-educated" about your own past.
- Other people begin repeating her version of events back to you.
- She refers to the past in ways that completely contradict your memory—and you're the only one who notices.

This is no accident. It's gaslighting taken to the narrative level.

What You Can Do

1. Keep Written Records

Document conversations, incidents, and dates. You're not being paranoid—you're reclaiming the truth.

1. Speak Your Truth, Even If You're the Only One

Don't let her control your voice. Write it. Speak it. Own it.

1. Limit Your Rebuttals

Trying to convince her—or those she's manipulated—is often pointless. Instead, focus on protecting your peace and surrounding yourself with reality-affirming people.

1. Validate Yourself Daily

Remind yourself: "Just because she said it, doesn't make it true."

The Bottom Line:

The female narcissist doesn't just want to control your behavior—she wants to own the story of who you are.
But here's the truth:

You are not the man she says you are.

You are not the villain in the story she tells.

You are not crazy.

You're just waking up to reality.
And that's exactly what she fears.

Step 5:
She Plays the Victim—Flawlessly

She may be the one who lied, manipulated, insulted, or abandoned you...

But somehow, by the time the dust settles—you're the villain, and she's the victim.

This isn't a mistake. It's her design.

The female narcissist thrives on control, and victimhood gives her the ultimate power: sympathy, deflection from blame, and weaponized protection from accountability.

Why She Chooses Victimhood

Playing the victim works incredibly well—especially for narcissistic women—because:

- Society is more likely to believe a woman who says she's been wronged.
- Most men are taught to avoid conflict, "be the bigger person," or walk away.
- Emotional pain in men is often dismissed, while emotional performance by women is often protected.

She knows this. She counts on it. And she wields it like a sword.

Rewriting Roles: Abuser as Victim

Here's how the female narcissist flips the narrative:

- She cheats → but says you drove her to it by being cold.
- She yells → but claims you scared her into a breakdown.
- She isolates you from friends/family → but tells others you're controlling and possessive.
- She abandons you emotionally → but insists you're the one who's unavailable.

She does this so convincingly—so emotionally and theatrically—that even you begin to question whether she might be right.

That's how powerful her performance is.

The Sympathy Stage

Female narcissists often go on what survivors call a "smear campaign"—a carefully constructed story they tell to friends, family, counselors, or even the court. In her version, she:

- "Tried everything to make the relationship work"
- "Was emotionally abused for years"
- "Felt trapped, alone, scared"
- "Put up with more than anyone ever should"

She cries. She trembles. She shakes her head in disbelief. And everyone believes her—because few expect that kind of performance from someone so dangerous behind closed doors.

Signs She's Playing the Victim

- She shares personal stories where she is always the one hurt—never the one who hurt.
- Her version of the past constantly paints you as "unstable," "cold," or "abusive."
- She tells others partial truths mixed with lies—making it harder for you to defend yourself.
- When you try to share your truth, she calls it "attacking" her or "smearing" her name.

Here's the twisted reality:

She'll do horrible things to you.

Then tell others you did them to her—with tears in her eyes.

Victimhood as a Cycle of Abuse

1. She harms you emotionally or verbally.
2. You call out the behavior.
3. She flips the script—accuses you of being cruel.
4. You defend yourself.
5. She escalates emotionally, cries, or plays fragile.
6. Others take her side, and you look like the aggressor.

This forces you into emotional silence. You stop speaking up. You start walking on eggshells. You question whether anyone will believe you.

And she thrives in that silence.

Why It's So Effective

Because she knows how to:

- Use language of pain and trauma to appear authentic.
- Exploit cultural sympathy for women in distress.
- Anticipate your defenses and turn them into new accusations.
- Cry on cue—often without feeling a thing.

In public, she's the fragile, mistreated partner. In private, she's the calculating manipulator.

And she's been perfecting this act her entire life.

How to Respond

1. Don't Play Into Her Frame

Don't argue with her narrative in front of others. Instead, calmly state your truth and let your consistency reveal her deception.

1. Document Everything

If you're in a divorce or custody battle, keep records of her behavior. Save messages. Write down conversations. The more she plays the victim, the more her inconsistencies will eventually show.

1. Protect Your Reputation Strategically

Share your truth with select, trusted individuals. Don't try to "clear your name" everywhere—that can backfire. Choose truth over noise.

1. Don't Take Her Bait

Her goal is to trigger you into a reaction that looks like aggression. Stay calm. That's your power.

1. Seek Validation from the Right Places

Not everyone will believe you. That's okay. Don't waste energy proving something to people who only know her mask. Focus on healing, not convincing.

Final Truth:

A female narcissist will set your life on fire—and then cry about how you made her burn.

Let her play the victim.

You focus on being the survivor.

Step 6:

Everyone Is a Pawn in Her Game

To the female narcissist, people aren't people—they're tools. Tools for admiration. Tools for manipulation. Tools for revenge. Everyone she interacts with has one purpose: to serve her agenda.

If you've ever felt like you were being played, used, or turned against... you were.

Because to her, relationships aren't about connection—they're about control.

The Master Manipulator

A female narcissist doesn't build relationships—she orchestrates alliances. Like a chess master, she positions people around her to protect her narrative, inflate her ego, or attack anyone who threatens her power.

You, her partner, are simply the king she wants on the board—until you become a liability. Then she turns others into pawns to isolate you, punish you, or replace you.

This manipulation isn't impulsive—it's strategic.

She uses charm, flattery, emotional stories, and victimhood to recruit allies—people who think they're supporting her, but are actually helping her control you.

Her Favorite Pawns

1. Your Friends

She flatters them, then slowly poisons them against you:

"He doesn't tell you everything, does he?"

"He's been acting really off lately."

"I just wish he were more open like you."

1. Her Friends

She uses them as a witness pool, people who will defend her no matter what. She often shares half-truths or lies about your relationship to earn their loyalty.

1. Your Family

She may initially be overly warm, then suddenly distant—claiming they're "toxic" or "interfering." Before long, she'll drive a wedge between you and the people who truly care.

1. Your Children

In family dynamics, narcissistic mothers or stepmothers can use children as emotional shields, messengers, or bargaining chips in custody or manipulation battles.

1. Therapists or Counselors

Yes, even professionals can be deceived. She'll present herself as vulnerable, wounded, and committed—while portraying you as closed-off, angry, or resistant.

1. The Court System

If divorce or custody is involved, she'll portray herself as the loving mother or victimized wife—while painting you as unstable, dangerous, or neglectful.

Triangulation: Her Most Common Game

Triangulation is the act of using a third person to control or manipulate the person she's targeting.

Example:

- She talks to her ex and says, "He still wants me back. I just don't know what to do."
- She texts your friend about a fight between you two.
- She compares you to another man: "At least he listens."

The goal? To:

- Make you feel jealous, paranoid, or insecure.
- Provoke a reaction she can use against you.
- Position herself as the center of attention and power.

She thrives when you're competing for her validation.

Signs You're Just One Piece on Her Board

- You feel constantly compared to others.
- She shares private relationship matters with people you both know.
- People seem to have strong opinions about you—based on things you never said or did.
- She keeps "confidants" who reinforce her victim story and attack your character.
- You feel like you're being judged by an invisible jury.

The truth? You are.

Because she's controlling the courtroom—and she made herself the innocent plaintiff before you ever knew there was a case.

How to Disengage from Her Game

1. Remove Yourself from Her Triangle

Refuse to compete, compare, or defend. Say:

"I'm not playing that game."

"This is between us—not your ex, not your friend, not your therapist."

1. Expose the Pattern, Not the Person

Trying to "out" her manipulation often backfires—especially with her pawns. Instead, privately state the behavior pattern:

"When you involve other people in our issues, it erodes trust."

Keep it calm. Keep it factual.

1. Cut Off Her Access to Allies

If possible, create emotional and communication boundaries. Limit her ability to gather intel, twist the story, or poison your support system.

1. Strengthen Your Own Circle

Build a network of people who know you, not her. Avoid oversharing, but be honest. The more grounded you are in truth, the less influence she has.

1. Don't Try to Win the Game

The only winning move is not to play. You can't out-manipulate a narcissist. You can only refuse to be controlled.

Final Truth:

The female narcissist doesn't want partnership. She wants a stage.

And everyone in her life is cast in a role—friend, rival, cheerleader, scapegoat, hero, villain.

You don't have to be in her play anymore.

Walk off the stage. Burn the script. Take back your story.

Step 7:

The Closer You Get, the Colder She Turns

You gave her everything—your time, your attention, your loyalty.

At first, she soaked it up like sunshine. She made you feel chosen. Desired. Special.

But then something changed.

The more you gave, the more distant she became.

The more available you were, the more contempt she showed.

And now? You're in the same room—but it feels like you're invisible.

This is the final, cruel pattern of the female narcissist: emotional abandonment once control is secured.

The Emotional Temperature Drop

In the early stages, she was all warmth and affection. You felt like you had finally found someone who truly saw you.

But now?

- She pulls away during conversations.
- She shows no interest in your emotions or achievements.
- She avoids intimacy—or uses it to manipulate.
- She criticizes your efforts instead of appreciating them.

You ask what's wrong. She shrugs.

You try to fix things. She rolls her eyes.

You remind her of how close you once were. She says you're "too needy."

The woman who once chased your attention now punishes you for offering it.

Why?

Because she already owns you. And once the narcissist feels total control, your value as a source of admiration plummets.

Idealize - Devalue - Discard

This is the classic narcissistic abuse cycle, and it ends in a cold void where love once was.

1. Idealize – She made you feel like the most important person on Earth.
2. Devalue – Subtle put-downs, passive aggression, emotional withdrawal.
3. Discard – Emotional or physical abandonment—often without warning.

And sometimes, just to maintain control, she'll hoover you back in—offering a brief return to the "ideal" stage—before the cycle restarts.

Signs You're in the Devaluation Phase

- She rarely initiates affection, but gets irritated if you stop trying.
- She avoids meaningful conversation.
- She finds fault with nearly everything you do.
- She accuses you of being distant or cold—despite her disconnection.
- You feel more alone with her than you would being single.

This is not relationship fatigue. It's not growing apart.
It's calculated emotional starvation.
She withholds love because it keeps you chasing.
And while you're chasing, she maintains power.

Why She Turns Cold

1. To Punish Your Intimacy

Emotional closeness requires vulnerability—and narcissists fear vulnerability. When you get too close, she lashes out or detaches.

1. To Keep You Off-Balance

Unpredictability keeps you anxious, which keeps you compliant.

1. To Make You Desperate

Withholding affection creates a craving that makes you work harder to please her.

1. To Justify Her Exit

Once she's ready to move on, she emotionally checks out first—so you look like the one who gave up.

What This Does to You

- You begin to feel invisible.
- You question your worth.
- You over-function, trying to fix what you didn't break.
- You feel like you're walking through an emotional desert while holding out water she refuses to drink.

This phase of the relationship is often the most painful—not because of what she does, but because of what she no longer does. The silence. The apathy. The absence of love.

How to Break Free from the Freeze

1. Stop Chasing Connection

You cannot fix what she is withholding on purpose. Step back. Observe. Reclaim your emotional energy.

1. Document the Shift

Record changes in her tone, behavior, and engagement. This helps clarify that you're not imagining things—it really did change.

1. Rebuild Self-Validation

Find ways to reconnect to yourself outside the relationship: hobbies, friends, therapy, spiritual grounding. You are not what she withholds.

1. Don't Accept Blame for Her Withdrawal

She may say "you changed." But no—she always planned to withdraw once she had control. This was not about your behavior. It was about her manipulation.

The Final Truth:

You loved her deeply.

She used your love until it bored her, burdened her, or threatened her control.

Then she withdrew it—not because of anything you did, but because that's who she is.

You didn't fail her.

She failed love.

And now it's time to choose yourself.

Red Flags Checklist: 30 Signs You're Dealing with a Female Narcissist

This chapter gives you the clearest, quickest reference to determine if the woman in your life exhibits narcissistic patterns. These aren't occasional bad behaviors—they're habitual, harmful traits that form a consistent pattern of manipulation, control, and emotional abuse.

If you recognize 10 or more of these red flags in your relationship, it's time to take a serious look at what's really going on.

Early-Stage Red Flags

These often appear during the first few weeks or months of dating:

1. She moves the relationship forward extremely fast.

Love bombing, constant attention, and premature talk of commitment.

1. She mirrors your interests and values almost perfectly.

She's everything you've ever wanted—suspiciously so.

1. She talks badly about all her exes.

Everyone else was "crazy," "abusive," or "never appreciated her."

1. She has few or no long-term friendships.

Especially with other women—because people eventually see through her.

1. She gets irritated when you set boundaries.

Even small boundaries are seen as rejection.

1. She needs constant attention and validation.

If you pull away or have other priorities, she accuses you of "not caring."

1. She complains that you're "too sensitive."

Especially after saying something cruel or disrespectful.

Mid-Stage Red Flags

These appear once you're emotionally invested:

1. She criticizes or mocks you in subtle ways.

Often in front of others, but disguised as "jokes."

1. She changes the story when confronted.

Gaslights you, denies things she said, or claims you misunderstood.

1. She controls your time, friends, or habits.

She wants full access to your schedule—and disapproves of any time spent without her.

1. She emotionally withdraws to punish you.

You upset her? Suddenly she's silent, cold, or distant.

1. She starts comparing you to others.

"He would never treat me this way" or "Why can't you be more like..."

1. She creates conflict out of thin air.

You walk on eggshells not knowing what will trigger her next.

1. She expects praise for basic decency.

Helping with chores or not yelling is portrayed as sainthood.

1. She plays the victim whenever you express your needs.

Suddenly you're the selfish one.

1. She violates your privacy.

Reads your messages, checks your location, monitors your habits.

1. She turns people against you.

Tells others partial truths or lies to control how they see you.

Late-Stage Red Flags

These emerge when the relationship is deteriorating—or you begin to pull away:

1. She discards you without warning or explanation.

Cold, cruel, and quick—often as if the love never existed.

1. She starts a smear campaign.

Tells mutual friends and family that you were "abusive," "unstable," or "narcissistic."

1. She uses the legal system as a weapon.

In divorce or custody battles, she plays the wounded party while lying to the court.

1. She manipulates your children or stepchildren.

Uses them as pawns to punish or control you.

1. She immediately replaces you with a new "perfect partner."

You're erased and replaced—overnight.

1. She pretends to want reconciliation—then punishes you for taking her back.

2. She denies the past.

Says things like: "That never happened," "You're making that up," or "You've always been like this."

1. She minimizes your pain.

Tells you to "get over it," "man up," or "stop being dramatic."

1. She claims she's the one healing from you.
2. She accuses you of doing the very things she does.

Projection is her favorite tactic.

1. She rewrites the story of your entire relationship.

You went from "soulmate" to "monster"—with no in-between.

1. She shows no remorse.

Her final act is indifference—or worse, smug satisfaction.

Final Word on Red Flags:

A few red flags might signal immaturity.

But a pattern of red flags reveals a narcissistic predator.

Your gut already knows

This checklist confirms it.

The Emotional Fallout: What Happens to You

Surviving a relationship with a female narcissist doesn't end the moment you leave her.

In many ways, that's when the real damage becomes clear.

You walk away—shaken, confused, and questioning everything. You may not have physical bruises, but emotionally, you feel battered. This is the silent devastation that narcissistic abuse causes, especially when it comes from a woman society expects to be nurturing, empathetic, and supportive.

This chapter explores what happens to you after narcissistic abuse—and why your pain is not only real, but often misunderstood.

The Invisible Wounds

Narcissistic women specialize in psychological erosion, not obvious attacks. And because the abuse is hidden behind smiles, charm, and plausible deniability, the damage goes unnoticed—especially by others.

But you feel it in ways no one can see:

- You no longer trust your instincts.
- You over-apologize, even when you're not wrong.
- You walk on emotional eggshells in every relationship.
- You hesitate to speak up or express needs.
- You feel unworthy of love.

This is what happens when you're trained to believe that your thoughts, feelings, and boundaries are invalid.

The Psychological Effects

Here's how long-term exposure to narcissistic abuse affects your emotional and mental health:

1. Chronic Self-Doubt

You were constantly told you "overreacted" or "misremembered." Now, even without her, you struggle to believe your own judgment.

2. Hypervigilance

You scan every situation for conflict. You feel unsafe even in safe environments. Your nervous system is always in defense mode.

3. Depression

The emotional isolation, repeated betrayals, and gaslighting drain you. Many survivors feel numb, hopeless, or emotionally shut down.

4. Anxiety and Panic

Especially when faced with confrontation, rejection, or being misunderstood. The fear of "doing something wrong" becomes overpowering.

5. Shame

You wonder how you could've been "so blind." You blame yourself for staying. But that shame is a symptom of the abuse—not a reflection of your worth.

6. Emotional Flashbacks

Even years later, hearing a certain tone of voice or being accused unfairly can send you spiraling. These aren't overreactions—they're trauma responses.

The Identity Crisis

One of the most devastating effects is this:

You lose yourself.

After months or years of walking on eggshells, changing who you are to survive, and being told you're "too much" or "not enough," you no longer recognize the man in the mirror.

You ask:

- Who am I now?
- Was I really the problem?
- Will I ever feel safe in love again?

These questions haunt survivors—especially men—because our culture teaches men to "toughen up," not to process grief, betrayal, and emotional trauma.

But you must process it. Otherwise, the abuse continues to control you—even in her absence.

Why Others Don't Understand

This kind of abuse is subtle, private, and often denied by the abuser. People may say:

- "She seems so sweet."
- "Are you sure you're not just bitter?"
- "Why didn't you leave sooner?"

Their confusion adds to your shame—and keeps many men suffering in silence.

That's why this book exists.

To validate what you already feel.

To say what so few others will:

Yes, she hurt you. Yes, you're allowed to say it. And yes, your healing matters.

You May Also Experience:

- Emotional numbness – You feel disconnected from joy, excitement, or love.
- Avoidant behavior – You isolate or sabotage relationships to avoid being vulnerable again.
- Repetition – You attract similar women again, hoping to "fix" the past by replaying it.
- Addictions or compulsions – To escape the inner pain, some survivors turn to substances, workaholism, or obsessive distractions.
- Self-silencing – You don't speak up anymore. You fear your voice will be used against you.

What You Can Do to Begin Healing

1. Name the Abuse

Call it what it was. Don't minimize it. Don't make excuses for her. This was not a "toxic relationship." This was emotional abuse.

1. Rebuild Your Identity

Journaling, therapy, and talking to safe people help you rediscover who you are without her voice in your head.

1. Feel What You Were Not Allowed to Feel

Grieve. Rage. Cry. Mourn the years lost and the version of yourself that was hidden to survive.

1. Join a Men's Recovery Group

There are communities of male survivors of narcissistic abuse who know exactly what you're going through. You are not alone.

1. Set New Standards

Final Truth:

Surviving her was only the first step.
    Healing from her is the real journey.
You will question yourself. You will hurt. You will grieve.
But you will also rebuild.
And when you do—you'll never mistake control for love again.

How to Escape with Your Sanity Intact

Leaving a narcissistic woman isn't like walking away from a normal relationship.

It's like escaping a psychological trap—one that's designed to keep you confused, entangled, and emotionally dependent.

She doesn't want you to leave.

She wants to leave you—on her terms, in her timing, and only after she's dismantled your confidence and rewritten the story.

So when you take back control? She will fight—dirty.

This chapter isn't just about walking away.

It's about escaping with your sanity, dignity, and identity still intact.

Know This First: She Will Not Let You Go Easily

When you start to pull away, expect one (or more) of the following:

- Rage – Explosive accusations, yelling, threats, or destruction of property.
- Tears – Desperate pleas, sobbing, and promises to change.
- Seduction – Sudden reappearance of love bombing and affection.
- Blame – Calling you a narcissist, an abuser, or a quitter.
- Smear Campaign – Telling everyone she left you because you were emotionally unstable.

This is all meant to pull you back in. Not because she loves you—but because she refuses to lose control.

The Psychological Hooks You Must Break

1. Guilt

She'll remind you of all she "did for you," even if you carried most of the weight. Guilt is her favorite leash.

1. Hope

She may act like the woman you wish she was—temporarily. But that version is a mask.

1. Fear

Of being alone, of being disbelieved, of financial or legal consequences. She knows how to push your buttons.

1. Confusion

She'll distort the truth until you're unsure of who's really at fault. That fog is part of her plan.

You must get crystal clear on one truth: You are not crazy. You are being controlled.

Step-by-Step: How to Leave a Female Narcissist Safely

1. Stop Arguing—Start Preparing

Don't announce your plans. Don't threaten to leave. Just quietly prepare:

- Gather financial records, legal documents, and personal belongings.
- Consult a lawyer or therapist before you leave.
- Secure passwords, accounts, and communications.

2. Build a Support System

Isolation is her power. Connection is yours.

- Confide in 1–3 people who will believe you and support you.
- Join online or in-person support groups for survivors of narcissistic abuse.

3. Go "Grey Rock"

Once you've emotionally disengaged, don't give her energy to feed on.

- Be boring, neutral, and unreactive.
- No defending, no explaining, no emotional responses.
- This protects your peace and denies her fuel.

4. Set Unbreakable Boundaries

- No more second chances.
- No contact (or low contact, if children are involved).
- Communicate only through written, trackable channels.

5. Expect Retaliation—Plan for It

- Save all messages.
- Document threats or manipulation.
- Be prepared for false accusations or sudden reversals of blame.

Practical Tips for a Clean Break

- Use written communication only. Never say something in person you can't prove later.
- Avoid "closure" conversations. She doesn't want closure—she wants control.
- Notify banks, credit cards, and shared accounts. Remove access, change passwords.
- Stay calm and consistent. She will bait you. Don't bite.

What You'll Feel After You Leave

- Relief—but also grief.
- Empowered—but also exhausted.
- Free—but also lost.

These emotions are normal. You're detoxing from psychological abuse.

You may feel tempted to return just to end the chaos. But remember: Peace is not the absence of conflict with her—it's the absence of her.

One Important Note: If You Share Children

- Never badmouth her in front of the kids.
- Document all interactions.
- Use parenting apps or court-ordered communication tools.
- Stay consistent, grounded, and calm.
- Keep your focus on protecting your children—not punishing her.

Final Truth:

Leaving her is not weakness.
It's strength. It's survival. It's rebirth.
You may walk away bruised—but you will walk away.
And what you reclaim in yourself is worth everything she took.

When the Courts Don't See Her Clearly

You've made the bravest choice: to walk away.

But what happens when she takes the fight to the courtroom?

For many men, the most devastating chapter of narcissistic abuse begins not at home—but in court. The woman who lied, gaslit, and manipulated behind closed doors now stands in front of a judge—calm, and prepared, to begin her "victim role".

She looks like a victim.

She sounds like a wounded mother or betrayed wife.

And suddenly... you're on trial not just for the relationship—but for your character.

This chapter prepares you for the hardest battle: when the system doesn't see her mask—and punishes you for it.

Why Courts Struggle to Spot Female Narcissists

1. Narcissistic women are excellent performers.

They know how to cry on cue, present as composed, and tell a compelling story.

1. Courts are biased toward protecting women and mothers.

Especially in family court, men are often presumed guilty—until proven innocent.

1. Emotional abuse is hard to prove.

There are no bruises. Just patterns. And narcissists erase or distort the record before it ever reaches a courtroom.

1. Documentation favors the loudest storyteller.

If she's prepared with screenshots, tearful declarations, and rehearsed anecdotes—while you're stunned and reactive—the system believes her.

The Narcissist's Legal Playbook

Here's how a female narcissist typically manipulates the court system:

- Filing first to frame the narrative early.
- Accusing you of abuse—emotional, physical, or even sexual.
- Crying in front of the judge to appear vulnerable.
- Dragging out proceedings to exhaust you financially and emotionally.
- Alienating your children to win full custody.
- Demanding alimony or assets as "compensation" for their suffering.
- Using your reactions against you. If you get angry, upset, or defensive—she points to that as "evidence."

And the worst part? It works far too often.

What You Must Do to Protect Yourself

1. Document EVERYTHING

- Save texts, voicemails, and emails.
- Screenshot threats, contradictions, and emotional manipulation.
- Record changes in behavior, especially around custody or finances.

2. Use Court-Recognized Communication Tools

- Apps like OurFamilyWizard or TalkingParents provide a secure, documented trail.
- Avoid phone or in-person conversations without witnesses.

3. Stay Calm, Even When It Hurts

- Judges don't see the past—they see the courtroom.
- The calmer you are, the more credible you appear.

4. Have a Lawyer Who Understands Narcissistic Abuse

- Not all attorneys do. Ask if they've handled high-conflict personalities or abuse-by-manipulation cases.
- Consider using a guardian ad litem or evaluator who can observe her directly.

5. Reframe the Narrative

- Focus on facts, not feelings.
- Use language like "consistent emotional instability," "documented control tactics," and "pattern of manipulation."

What Not to Do

- Don't explode. One emotional outburst can undo months of preparation.
- Don't rely on others to "see her true colors." Many won't.
- Don't try to out-manipulate her. Stay in the truth—always.

If Children Are Involved

This is where her cruelty may peak. She'll:

- Use your children as leverage.
- Try to turn them against you.
- Undermine your role as a father.
- Accuse you of neglect or abuse.

Your best response?

- Document her actions, not just your own.
- Continue showing up for your children, even if they've been turned against you.
- Speak with attorneys, therapists, and court evaluators about parental alienation—a real and recognized tactic narcissists use.

The Mental Toll

It's easy to feel hopeless.

You did everything right. You left the abuse.

And now you're in a system where the abuser is rewarded—and you're punished.

But here's the truth:

You are not powerless.

The law may be slow. The court may be blind.

But the truth—documented, repeated, calmly presented—has a way of shining through.

Final Truth:

You're not fighting for revenge.
You're fighting for freedom, fairness, and your future.
The courtroom is not the end.
It's just another obstacle on your road to peace.
Hold your ground.
Guard your mind.
And don't let her story become your sentence.

Final Words: You Are Not Alone

If you've made it to this chapter, you've already taken the first—and hardest—step:

You've named the truth.

You've admitted what so many men are shamed into silence about:

That you loved someone who slowly, methodically, and often cruelly broke you down.

You loved a woman who didn't love you—she loved power.

And once she got it, she used it to rewrite the story, erase your worth, and leave you questioning everything.

But that doesn't define you.

What defines you is this:

You saw the truth.

You survived the confusion.

And now, you're ready to rebuild.

If You're Still With Her

You may still be caught in the cycle. You may be planning your exit. As I was.

You may still wake up each morning trying to "fix things" or wondering if you're overreacting.

You're not.

If you had to read this book in secret, if you nod through the pages feeling seen for the first time in years—you already know.

You're not weak. You're not dramatic.

You're being emotionally and psychologically abused.

You deserve better.

If You've Already Left

You may feel lost. Lonely. Ashamed that you stayed so long. Angry that no one believed you.

That's okay.

Healing isn't a straight line. Some days you'll feel strong. Other days, you'll question everything again. But the longer you stay away, the louder your own voice becomes.

And eventually, you'll hear yourself again.

If You Ever Doubt Yourself Again...

Come back to these truths:

- Real love doesn't confuse you.
- Real love doesn't drain you.
- Real love doesn't mock, manipulate, or discard you.
- You are not crazy. You are recovering.

And most of all:

You are not alone.

There are millions of men like us—intelligent, successful, good-hearted men—who got caught in the web of a female narcissist. It doesn't make you weak.

It makes you human.

And now it makes you free.

Author's Statement

I didn't write this book as a therapist.

I wrote it as a man who nearly lost himself loving the wrong woman.

My name is Dr. Paul J. Peloquin Sr., PhD. And I know firsthand what it feels like to be silenced, dismissed, and misunderstood by people who don't see the private side of the woman you loved.

I wrote "How to Identify a Female Narcissist in 7 Steps" for every man who walked through that fire. Whether you're still in it, barely out, or far down the road of recovery—I want you to know:

You are not crazy.

You are not broken.

And you are not alone.

I dedicate this book to the silent warriors. The men who stayed too long. The men who believed the best. The men who lost themselves but started finding their way back. Most of all the support network you create and the support you receive. (Annie, Zach, Hunter, Joey)

Keep going.

You are worth saving.

— Dr. Paul J. Peloquin Sr., PhD

Front Cover – Text Layout

Title:
How to Identify a Female Narcissist in 7 Steps
A Survivor's Guide for Men
Byline:
Dr. Paul J. Peloquin Sr., PhD

Back Cover Text

BACK COVER COPY:

She was charming, magnetic, and impossible to resist—until she wasn't.

Behind the smile was manipulation. Behind the affection, control. And behind the relationship, a war you never saw coming.

In How to Identify a Female Narcissist in 7 Steps, I expose the hidden traits of female narcissists and the emotional damage they inflict on unsuspecting men. Drawing from personal experience and professional insight, I offers a powerful, step-by-step guide to help men recognize the red flags, escape the manipulation, and reclaim their sanity.

Whether you're still in the relationship, recovering from it, or trying to make sense of the chaos—it's time to break the silence.

This book will help you:

- Spot narcissistic red flags early
- Understand the psychological traps used to control you
- Escape without losing your dignity or mind
- Rebuild your identity after narcissistic abuse
- Realize you are not alone—and never were

You're not overreacting. You're waking up.
And this guide will help you stay awake.

Back Cover – Short Author Bio

About the Author

Dr. Paul J. Peloquin Sr., PhD is a behavioral expert, trainer, and survivor of narcissistic abuse, Founder of 'The American Board of Certified Interventionists, (Recognized as the Pioneer of Interventionists certification), Alabama Council on Pathological Gambling, With decades of professional experience and hard-won personal insight, he helps men recognize and escape the grip of emotionally manipulative women. My mission is to break the silence around male victims of abuse—and provide the tools for lasting healing.

He lives in South Florida, where he writes, mentors, and speaks truth with a margarita in hand and no cigarette in other (I stopped smoking 10 years after starting at 55 brought on by the ex. And on the behalf of those still trying to be heard You will Know when...

Inside Page – Full Author Bio (for "About the Author" section)

About the Author

Dr. Paul J. Peloquin Sr., PhD is a behavioral and training professional with a deeply personal mission: to expose the hidden face of narcissistic abuse inflicted by women—and to give men the strength and clarity to escape it. After surviving a 15-year relationship with a narcissistic partner, Dr. Peloquin chose to turn his pain into purpose by writing a series of books that speak directly to male survivors.

With decades of experience in leadership, mentoring, and psychological training, his insights are grounded not only in academic understanding—but in lived experience. His writing combines emotional truth with practical tools to help men recognize manipulation, recover their confidence, and rebuild their lives.

Dr. Peloquin continues to write and advocate for men's emotional health from his home in Florida. His work empowers those who have suffered in silence to finally speak up—and never be silenced again. With a strong hope that just one person reads this book and the others, and it saves him by waking up to those hidden facts. You just can see.

The End

Don't miss out!

Visit the website below and you can sign up to receive emails whenever Dr Paul J Peloquin Sr, PhD publishes a new book. There's no charge and no obligation.

https://books2read.com/r/B-A-URIYD-GOYJG

BOOKS 2 READ

Connecting independent readers to independent writers.

About the Author

From Dr. Paul J. Peloquin Sr., PhD

This book was born out of silence.

Not the kind that comforts—but the kind that crushes. The kind that creeps into your life when you're too ashamed to speak. When you're too afraid to be disbelieved. When you've been told—over and over again—that your truth is not valid, your pain is not real, and your story is not worth telling.

I wrote Echoes of Control to prove that it is.

For years, I lived behind closed doors, enduring subtle manipulations and outright cruelty at the hands of a woman who wore a mask so well the world applauded while I quietly withered. I doubted myself. I questioned my worth. And I stayed longer than I should have—not out of weakness, but out of hope, loyalty, and the belief that love should be enough.

But some love isn't love. It's control. And some people don't want connection—they want submission.

This book is not a revenge story. It is a resurrection story.

Every chapter is a declaration: that men can be victims. That narcissistic abuse is real. That emotional trauma leaves scars just as deep as physical ones. And that no matter how long you've lived in darkness, the light is still yours to claim.

If you're reading this and you feel seen, I hope you also feel strengthened.

If you're reading this and you've survived something similar, I hope you feel validated.

And if you're still in the fog—I hope this book is your first glimpse of clarity.

You are not crazy.

You are not weak.

And you are not alone.

This is the NEW not the old normal...

– Dr. Paul J. Peloquin Sr., PhD

www.ingramcontent.com/pod-product-compliance
Lightning Source LLC
LaVergne TN
LVHW090422210926
848480LV00002B/648
9798231871063